DISNEY

ZOOTOPIA

pi kids®   phoenix international publications, inc.

Judy Hopps has dreamed about being a cop ever since she was a little bunny. She just graduated from the police academy and is starting her new life in Zootopia, where anyone can be anything!

As Hopps takes in the bright lights of the big city, can you find her and these Zootopian citizens?

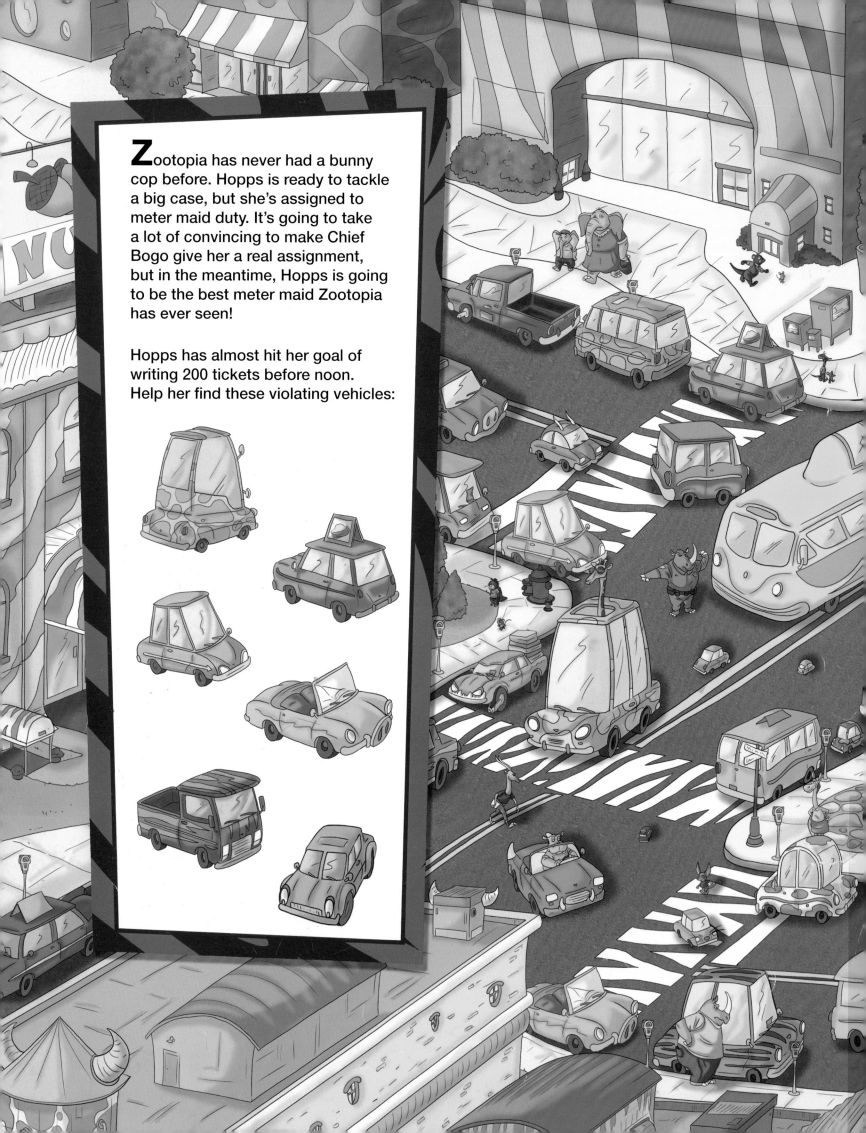

Zootopia has never had a bunny cop before. Hopps is ready to tackle a big case, but she's assigned to meter maid duty. It's going to take a lot of convincing to make Chief Bogo give her a real assignment, but in the meantime, Hopps is going to be the best meter maid Zootopia has ever seen!

Hopps has almost hit her goal of writing 200 tickets before noon. Help her find these violating vehicles:

While keeping the peace at Jumbeaux's Café, Hopps meets Nick Wilde, a fox who's always working on a new "hustle." With his partner Finnick posing as a toddler, Nick tricks Hopps into buying them an ice pop big enough for an elephant. It's the last trick he'll play on her!

See if you can find these zoo-per size desserts:

Assistant Mayor Bellwether helps Hopps get her first real case—the mysterious disappearance of Emmitt Otterton—but Chief Bogo gives her only two days to solve it. Hopps hustles Nick into being her partner, and they head to one of Emmitt's favorite places, the Mystic Spring Oasis, where animals "go natural."

Some Zootopians love to loosen up. Can you spot these poses?

Hopps gets a hot lead on a suspicious car and heads to the Department of Mammal Vehicles. Nick tells Hopps that his DMV buddy, Flash, can run the plate in a hurry. Little does Hopps know, DMV employees are all sloths—some of the slowest creatures ever!

Find these delayed DMV-goers, but not too fast! You've got plenty of time.

In the Rainforest District, Hopps questions a jaguar named Mr. Manchas, and he goes "savage," crouching on all fours and attacking with teeth and claws—something no upstanding Zootopian would ever do. Hopps and Nick need to escape before they're tropical toast!

Swing through the rainforest and try to pick out these awesome blossoms:

Hopps and Nick discover a secret lab where sheep create a serum used to make Zootopians go savage. Armed with evidence, they cut through the Natural History Museum where they're cornered by Assistant Mayor Bellwether. She's been using the serum to give predators a bad rap, and to get rid of Mayor Lionheart!

Locate these animal-mannequins in the Natural History Museum:

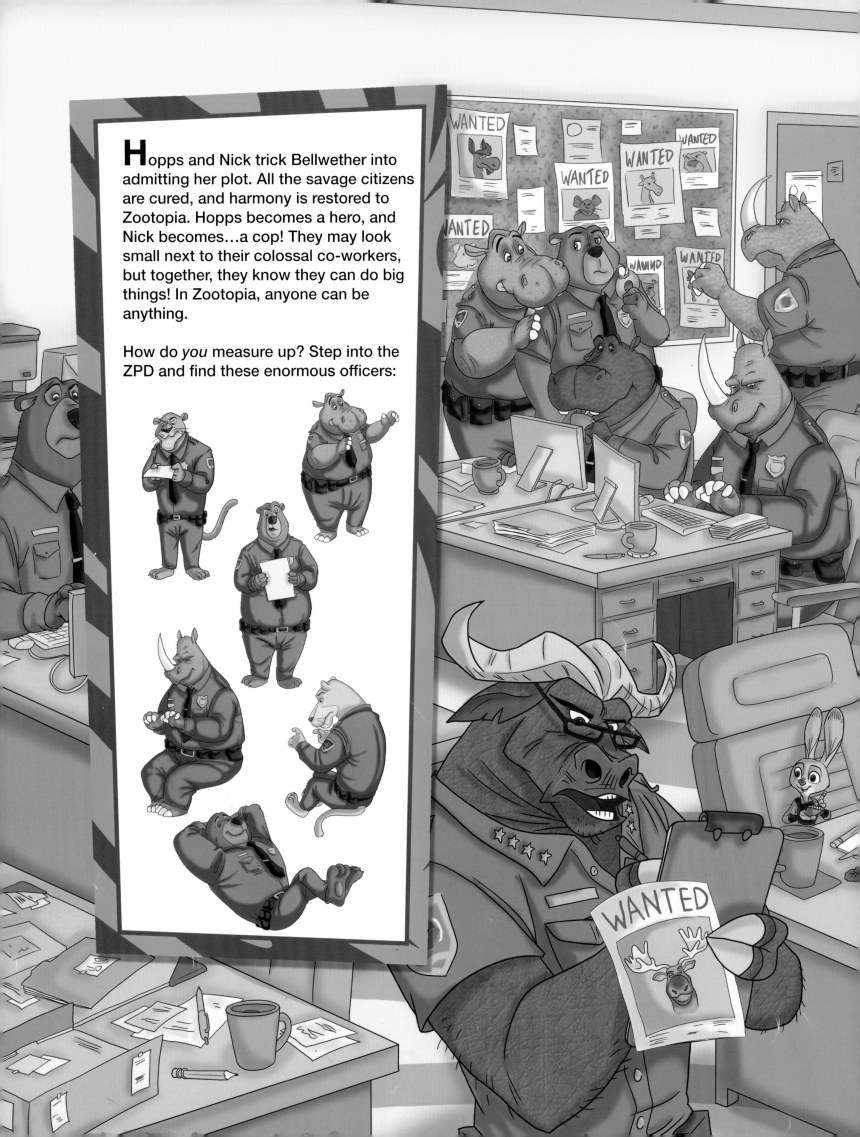

Hopps and Nick trick Bellwether into admitting her plot. All the savage citizens are cured, and harmony is restored to Zootopia. Hopps becomes a hero, and Nick becomes…a cop! They may look small next to their colossal co-workers, but together, they know they can do big things! In Zootopia, anyone can be anything.

How do *you* measure up? Step into the ZPD and find these enormous officers:

Can you find your way back to downtown Zootopia? Follow the signs:

VOTE

FLOCKING PROHIBITED

MAMMALS AT WORK

Jumbeaux's CAFE

OTTERTONS FLORIST SHOP

STAMPEDING

Scurry back to your meter before Hopps gives *you* a ticket! While you're at it, find these booted tires:

Hungry for more elephantine edibles? Head back to Jumbeaux's and spot these t-shirts while you wait in line:

Jumbo-pop

TUNDRATOWN

re-elect LEODORE

I ♥ ZOOTOPIA

Little Rodentia

Gazelle

Mindfully meander back to Mystic Spring Oasis and search for these super-natural items:

this yoga mat

water bottle

this yoga mat

candle

incense

dream catcher

Crawl back to the DMV and identify these ticking timepieces:

Run back to the rainforest and spy these hidden cameras scattered throughout the jungle:

Don't know much about history? Head back to the Natural History Museum and research these artifacts:

Slink back to the ZPD and find these posters of Zootopia's most wanted: